MW01502916

Deanna Moody was born and raised in Florida. She graduated from Ponte Vedra High School. Deanna has been writing poetry and short stories since December 2017 and enjoys the darker side of literature filled with plot twists and interesting storylines. Her writing style has been molded from her experiences with relationships with unkind people and giving hints as to how she moved past them.

This book is dedicated to all the people who have been torn apart from the people they care about. I am in awe of your tenacity to move forward and your optimism of finding the best you possibly can.

Deanna Moody

MISTAKES LIKE THIS

AUSTIN MACAULEY PUBLISHERS™

LONDON · CAMBRIDGE · NEW YORK · SHARJAH

Copyright © Deanna Moody 2023

All rights reserved. No part of this publication may be reproduced, distributed, or transmitted in any form or by any means, including photocopying, recording, or other electronic or mechanical methods, without the prior written permission of the publisher, except in the case of brief quotations embodied in critical reviews and certain other non-commercial uses permitted by copyright law. For permission requests, write to the publisher.

Any person who commits any unauthorized act in relation to this publication may be liable to criminal prosecution and civil claims for damages.

Ordering Information
Quantity sales: Special discounts are available on quantity purchases by corporations, associations, and others. For details, contact the publisher at the address below.

Publisher's Cataloging-in-Publication data
Moody, Deanna
Mistakes Like This

ISBN 9781647503949 (Paperback)
ISBN 9781649791153 (ePub e-book)

Library of Congress Control Number: 2023909882

www.austinmacauley.com/us

First Published 2023
Austin Macauley Publishers LLC
40 Wall Street,33rd Floor, Suite 3302
New York, NY 10005
USA

mail-usa@austinmacauley.com
+1 (646) 5125767

To friends of the past; if it wasn't for you, I never would have had the motivation to pick up my pencil and start writing. If you weren't there, I wouldn't be who I am today. You've taught me how to become stronger and learn how to fight for myself while also learning to love myself after many years of negativity. So even though I can never forgive you, I greatly thank you for being the reason I am able to keep writing. I hope you're living well.

Table of Contents

The One Who Forgets
Always Remembers

Strong winds blow through the forest inside my mind
Rushing through the tall trees
Swiftly erasing all my memories
Without you, I am everything but blind.

From happy to sad and good to bad
Washing out the image of the clown
Emotions and events being incinerated
Like a roach in the shower you drown.

The mask with the love falls to the ground
No longer am I your counselor
Skip away to the fantasy world
Bottom feeders have no meaning to the hustler.

Before you cry and before you beg
Tell yourself pretty lies
Distracted from the pain
The wind's almost through as that part of me dies.

Deleted and gone
You hold out your hand
Reaching for me so hard
I don't understand.

Finally flushed out
The circus left my town
Fun while it lasted
Excited, the tents were taken down.

No please, stay for the finale
One more taunt
This last entry
Listen while I debunk everything you want.

I am not you and you are not I
Conjoined we never were, just like the desert you are dry.

The Crowned, the Servant, and the Bystander

Once joined at the hip
All sharing the youth-filled belief
Of a life connected with happiness
Knowing none of their realties stuffed with grief.

The first blessed with knowledge
A boy small and dependable
Honest bystander, noble and pure
The crowned found him expendable.

Under his new mask
Lies a child grabbing for friends
Missing the ones who are missing
Ascend slowly or you'll get the bends.

The second graced with strength
Bonded to a selfish taker
A girl labeled a slave
The crowned used her as a caretaker.

Living present day wandering around
The unforgettable words of her protected
Grasping for a past that was never really there
No time for air when your seat is ejected.

At last, the time is here
We have reached the bottom
One last identity to reveal
A child brought up in autumn.

Continue cautiously
For his words run deep
Sprinkled with a brilliant passion
Keeping his true feelings in a locked-away heap.

The third and final, cursed with tenacity
A boy once full of life
Transformed to the crowned
The form he possess stabbed him with a laced knife.

Although it is sad to say
His crown remains atop his head
Sparkling with the tears of others
If only he could wake up in his old bed.

Tired and overrated
He softly screams his desire and places his label
Hands up and ready
As he throws the bystander across the table.

Issues from A to Z
The crowned is a true masterpiece
A diagram of what not to do
Once a wish of simple peace.

On that day, we all received a grim reminder
Masks crack and games end
Angry boys turn to puppet master men
To him their hearts they'd lend.

The truth untold
Playing with the future
He dips his words in our minds
We are the wound and he is the suture.

Please don't worry too much
His reign is almost over
Three years at most
The greatest interpersonal crossover.

Their lives continue today in mayhem
The crowned, the servant, and the bystander
It all started with a fight
Walls laced with candor.

A trio turned duo stands together in controlled sections
Even the closest of birds fly in different directions.

The Book of the Fallen

Within the shallow realm of our average minds
Lies a creature of a different face
For most, the being is microscopic and ineffective
For the chosen the being is stout, beest left for the chase.

A name and a face is all it takes
To make this world a better place
Don't fret, dear children
Your innocence shall keep your soul in space.

On a boring afternoon in the spring of 2006
A silhouette of a man with a being so well-defined appeared
The smile of a child while his insides were scrambled with
twisted desires
Take this new god's hand, don't be scared.

Heroes and villains become harder to tell apart
In one's heart, their actions graze the line of good and evil
While one child sits alone with a book in hand and murder
in thoughts
Vanquish the helpful mask and all that remains is the
smiling devil.

The end justifies the means, is what an honest man would say
How are you to kill the hidden joker with your hands unable to move?
The fear of his mesmerizing eyes paralyzes you
Determination is frightful, he has something to prove.

God was shot dead in his yellow box of misguided fortune
Two legends stripped from the worlds grasp
The years of their departure counting upwards
A concept a dimwit couldn't dream to clasp.

A trio of youngbloods hold his key qualities in their bones
The girl with passion, a male embodiment of the successor, and a carbon copy of the famous antagonist
Asking how I can take a side, just ask the shadow next to mine
Look deep into his eyes, and don't be extravagant.

A God upon legends is not easily replaced
With a scepter and crystal crown, sit still, your image is being traced.

Destined to Dance with You

Papers upon papers in the eternal flame
A choice that is not a choice but an order written in the sky
Scouring the sea searching for someone to blame
Nothing is permanent but the obvious goodbye.

The light to shine for all acts as the moon
For his beams are not his own, they are simple reflections
As the being sways too close to his destiny, the dance shall
come soon
While unaware of the unpredictable objections.

The concept called fate resides in the brain
If you do not show the child how to walk, they never will
Look to the deep phrases of the shadows to keep sane
How should we kill the figure that we cannot kill?

The boy of many faces sits in front
A catalyst made of glass resists the shatter
Years in a homely prison unable to hunt
What lies ahead of him can only be described as a shiny mad
hatter.

Acting like something you're not is a true bother
The mask can slip down so easily
In the state called zugzwang, who could place a single fother?
His people have no choice, he behaved quite treacherously.

Jump on in, say hello
Don't leave me alone tonight
For if you sink, we'll both go down below
Rip away the odds and do what is right.

Grab his hand and dance the destined dance
Go forward and show God even the hopeless have a chance.

Blame It on the Kids

Logistically, this was the only solution
Accusations made and tears flow down
Little kids ran for their lives
Fleeing from their once-stable town.

Over their heads
It doesn't matter how far you run
Those old regrets will never leave
Even whilst with your friends watching the dark sun.

Tonight, we serve pity for the few who've survived
Eat it well for it's all we've got
Make sure to savor every bite
Or else this was all for naught.

That smell seems familiar, doesn't it?
Ignorance and bliss are awfully similar
Love and hate too close to push apart
Parental figures turning into the horrid fiddler.

Trust is a substance never fully earned
Only a special type of liar can gain

Smiling faces can be happily torn to shreds
Have you yet to go insane?

The young children did doth square like warriors
Inching closer to the point of no return
Come out where your pretty face's hiding
No doubt many simple difficulties left to learn.

In order to assure the safety of the young
You must think the unthinkable thought
Grab hold of the power to harm and use it well
Quicker now, move your feet before you're caught.

A single king of spades rests at the peak
Grab him swiftly before he comes tumbling down
The drafty differences painted upon his soft skin
Rewrite fate and strip him of the brainwashing crown.

Coequal if 't be true the one on top forbids
Reacheth down deep to findeth thy heart, don't blame it on
the kids.

Don't Call the Paper-Faced Man

Twisted up smiles with shiny golden specks
Curious small beings with nowhere to go
Put on the happy mask and play outside
The paper-faced man knows all there is to know.

The phone will buzz and the dense will speak
Unknown, unknown pick up to play
Glass eyes upon a pasty shadow
Don't listen to the riddles, he'll say.

A past so obscure it's hard to believe
The paper-faced man has seen unimaginable things
Livestock in an old farm
Unspeakable baggage that man brings.

No features to notice no voice to hear
So obviously not obvious
A scream so silently loud
The only figure not remaining oblivious.

Pity strums heart strings
The new youth falls

Ignoring all the warnings
Don't answer when the paper-faced man calls.

Ring ring, hello?
Picking up the phone
He takes a long pause
Before he grabs you as his own.

As the room hushes, listen here
"Paper creases cannot be fixed until the sky is clear."

Wherefore Doth Thee Leaveth Me?

Grasp reality before it slips away
Grip it with all your strength
Helping my friends, forgetting the pain
Freedom just barely at arm's length.

Intellectual poster boy
Brains before beauty according to me
Described as a number
That's all I'll ever be.

In the darkest of rooms, I sit
Unable to move
Mother! Mother! Wherefore art thou, Mother?
Sitting up quickly, the dream was all there to prove.

For she is not here and she never will be
The graceful goddess listening to all except for I
I did caterwauling
Watch closely and try not to pry.

My mother, my mother
Where has she gone?
Over by the tree with one of the young
Staying away from dusk to dawn.

Understanding these actions I cannot do
I am her blood
And she'd dare let me die?
With her tears this farm shall flood.

My mother, my mother
Please comprehend my choices
Light the match and pour the gas
Perhaps this will stop those pesky voices.

Bon voyage! Goodnight, Mommy
See you in the midst of my sorrow-filled tsunami.

The Hardest of Simple Partings

Step into the mirror and you will find
Images of the old pair we used to be
The hopes and dreams destined to be declined
The former personas of you and me.

Years have passed and thoughts have slipped
That infamous coat and cap upon your body
The pool of false confidence where my toe remains dipped
A look that can only be described as gaudy.

The speech I must give
The words I must say
Without you, how was I to live?
Faceless marionettes in this despicable child's play.

Burned into my head remains the smile of their departings
This goodbye is surely the hardest of simple partings.

The King of Cardboards

Noble striped sweaters on white soft skin
Pretty deep eyes reflecting the image of innocence
The laughable theory of Malthus spun upside down
Wide beliefs used to jump the translucent fence.

The circular rings in our concentric zone model
Fields of grace placed in center
Profit goes up while mortality rate goes down
Come, come, into the twilight zone he shall enter.

A vessel without a brain is as a soup without a spoon
Ripped slowly, his mind switches back-and-forth
For how to flip a super glued switch
His old companions charging north.

Stay in your neuro-sector, defend it well
His words will seep through, infecting the head
Genocide is the answer, kill them all!
Silly godlike teen, it's time for bed.

Reigning over millions, power in his voice
A legacy could be created with a finger flick
The arm of paths stuck his head on, active
Midnight is close, hear that? *Tock tick.*

Why rule over cutouts, o' king of cardboards?
Dulce et Decorum est – don't take the servants, take the
lords.

Light

Everyone runs to the light
To feel like someone's at their side
It just looks so shiny and bright
But it gives away where the demons hide.

Then the light's mask begins to break
And all you can do is stare
As you realize the light was fake
And you feel completely bare.

You were sucked into the light's trap
There's no escape, it's already too late
As you feel your hopes snap
And you accept your fate.

No one ever comes to save the day
Because if they did, they might also stray away.

The Train That Goes Nowhere

The train that is going nowhere
Tells a familiar story
One to be told with care and grace
From the point of view of glory.

Take a minute, sit down
Shoes slip slowly off
A train rushes like a world class sprinter
The blockade of our fast-paced lives cause a simple cough.

Steam cascades off the colossal transporter
Phrases portrayed by Edward Hopper
The sky a matte dusty white
With grass appearing like copper.

At any time, the machine could halt
All passengers leap forward, *crash!*
But how could that possibly occur
If we are all stuck on permanent dash?

The wind whistled a sharp tune
As the railroad train stands still
So its fragile gears stop pumping
While our way of life takes away its moving will.

Go ahead, try to start it up
Give it a squeeze; give it a tug
There's no use in attempting
Go home and find something else to bug.

If only we could stop for one solid second
Just listen to the corporate songs beckon.

Ideals of the Mirrored Man

Nine long, repeating years
The same statements remain on play
Since when did you see us as foreign?
Resting upon false grass on that fated day?

Hours of pointless questions
Answers loaded with skills you lack
Staring off with that glossy look
All this time planning to fade to black.

How you look and how you feel
Are on complete opposite sides of the wall
Eyes with cataracts beyond recognition
Tell us how you gave it your all.

Backwards and foolish
Your mask makes absolutely no sense
Hiding behind expectations
Without a care in the world, jump the fence.

It's all clear now!
Your motives are as obvious as the sun
If this mirror didn't exist
Our worries could decrease to none.

Why do you concern yourself so much with me?
A man flipped truly upside down
Stuck on autopilot
With a superglued frown.

Don't wrap in with the mirrored man
His life is a fraud
Phrases disappear into thin air
Tissues placed in a manipulative wad.

Get out while you can, leave him behind
His confident sounds send us to a spinning rewind.

Paradox

One foot in front of the other
Step-by-step
This life seems too daunting
Try to stride with pep.

We all have a favorite
Do not deny
It's okay, I promise
All's well that ends well until you lie.

The people you hold onto
Let go
One action, one day
My own greatest foe.

Take it slow now
Don't be afraid of the dark
Everything shall be clear soon
Try not to flinch at the dog's bark.

Absurd while also humane
Place the fold upon glossy eyes
Stop moving
Say hello to the worst of goodbyes.

Trying to make sense
Of the madness in our heads
Stand still
Grab a handful of meds.

All the times I've opened up
You're the only one to see the real me
Look quickly now
It shall be the last you'll see.

We create the paradox of pleasure
Wrapped tight in our unconscious leisure.

Not My Wish but Yours

Conjoined only by blood
The most similar of differences
Memories that are not mine come and flood
Not my wish but yours.

Words of the past
Actions thought wrong turned right
Come see, quietly and fast
Not my wish but yours.

Standing with the mask of someone who understood
Taking me for a fool
Scowling under that oversized gray hood
Not my wish but yours.

My rage grows stronger
It's time we go
I will be ignored no longer
Not my wish but yours.

Back in time to that day
Can you see what I see?
Fathers changing course, what did you say?
Not my wish but yours.

What does this mean? What is there to do?
A family of monstrous mannequins
Brother, now you've abandoned me too
Not my wish but yours.

The words he said, the look on his face
Past events come back to the present
If only we knew our place
Not my wish but yours.

What do you want? Speak your wish
Freedom is so close and now you've done this
Serving stupidity on a golden dish
Not my wish but yours.

Sinking down while my mind pours
For the final time, not my wish but yours.

Gather for the Puppet Show

Ladies and gentlemen, welcome to the show!
Lodging thy glasses on and did shut thy mouth
Dark it must remain so the star may glow
Behold! A shadow of a shadow, peek-a-boo.

Confusion casts its way over her
Hast the lady madeth thee nimble-footed?
Get in line, fool, plenty have gone crazy from stir
The queen of kings hast nay useth f'r no more brain than
stone people.

You get what you paid for, this is quite the show
Laugher and smiles can be seen from backstage
On the edge of seats, spectators wait for the main blow
Strings lingering down from the black auditorium.

Young and menacing, her silhouette appears
The lady spoke w'rds only the roach couldst heareth
Air growing brisk as she swiftly nears
Dare to stare at the hard hitter.

You're still here? Just as planned
A warning unheeded, remember those words
Reality smacks like a back hand
Her façade rips to sheer terror.

Sociopathic beauty with ignorant pawns
Still not und'rstanding how nay one can seeth
Cruel and stoic while the dunce fawns
Silky strings strapped now to you
Lifting out of your seat, fear is clear
She's not real! She's not real!
Shout all you must for we are the only ones here
Are you enjoying the show?

This shouldst beest gross in sense but I'll sayeth 't again
Nev'r testeth and keepeth thy distance from the deceiv'r
thane.

How to Save a Life

Springing up to your feet
It's time to go now
Wipe away those tears feeling the facial heat
Mismatched clothes, you are me, how?

Switched at birth we always were
Oblivious and ignorant to the obvious
My wants created this horrid blur
Please return to the previous.

Begging and praying
Mother, don't do this
Evaporation leads my trust spraying
Cutthroat and kick me out of my bliss.

Blood of the innocent required for change
A change that is not a change but a façade
The feeling called happiness oh so strange
Golden shadow I awed.

Turn back and face your fear
She stands alongside you eternally
Shouting, shouting, can you not hear?
Making wounds externally.

This whole scenario arises one question
Burning our heads from start to stop
Own up and give us your confession
Sit here with a little *plop*.

How to save a life is simple and plain
Slip the right words, make the right face, ease out and enchain.

Legends Never Die

Everything starts with a question
But the biggest and broadest one of all
Is made of the simplest of words and phrases
Will you be able to answer it?

Begging for the silhouette's approval
Crying at the figure's feet
From above looking like a pathetic fool
Get off the ground now, child.

Come this way and you'll see
Nothing means anything
Make your own rules
Be the you, you were destined to be.

Don't cry and don't whine
We don't care about your feelings
Worrying and wondering
Are time consumers to mankind?

There is no answer to a question that hasn't been asked
So here is the tongue twister of a lifetime
Are you able to leave yourself behind?
I'll give you some time to think about it.

I gave my answer long ago
Without even thinking
I threw away my humanity
To become something more than myself.

The devil and I are one in the same
And so could the two of us
Say yes and your future is set
Say no and I'm sure it'll be an instant regret.

We'll wait for your answer
But don't take too long
Soon we will find another
So hurry before you're forgotten again.

The most convincing liars never lie
Heroes are remembered but legends never die.

Lone Warrior

In a little room
Chains fall over her
She rests in her crystal tomb
Her face a pale blur.

The tears seen from her eyes
As the prison formed
Surrounded by her lies
The soldiers swarmed.

Frozen in place
Tears stained forever
Floating in deep space
Unable to reach the lever.

Pessimists and pricks
Destroying her good name
Words break souls not sticks
She had perfect aim.

Needing no time
She is graceful
A goddess so divine
Getting rid of her, how wasteful.

Her friends and comrades now gone
She rests alone
Like a black swan
With a screaming tone.

The screech of her form
Beckoned them here
A perfect storm
View nice and clear.

She knows not
Of what has become of her world
Her partners were caught
While she sits in her ball curled.

An innocent flashback
With her undefeated kick
Her unseen attack
Hanging onto life like a tick.

Do not underestimate
The beautiful things
Or a despicable fate
Decides the song death sings.

Isolation and silence
Are all she has
Even with her current absence
She will not spaz.

Listen closely and you will learn
The lone warrior will one day return.

Do You Know the Boy of Many Faces?

An angry, unintimidating little boy
The undesirable traits that lie within him
A face which cries a mural of events
Eyes that speak small speeches of freedom.

Clattered bears with two porridge bowls left
The young trapped under layers of expectations
Supposed hope of humanity abandoning his flock
Running with his cracked new face of stupidity.

Power so easy to harm and uses well
Underneath the stoic wall lie a sobbing fool
A dictator with a soul can only ever be a proxy
Fade away, little boy, your faces are beginning to show.

Mother and father will never return
The boy pushes his closest so far
For their safety or to boost his fragile ego?
Caught in the maelstrom of his own words.

The boy of many faces
Is blind to his own visions
Wallowing in the misery he created
Crying edible tears for the new youth to soak up.

The boy of many faces collapses in on himself
Faces fold and shut him out, he was nothing more than a
puppet on a shelf.

Mind and Body

Here lies the body
Of a once-happy girl
Turned evil by her own head
Sending her life into a chaotic swirl.

Physically, she is not dead
But her presence is equivalent with that of a ghost
Standing in transparent ways
I miss her the most.

We would frolic and share thoughts
Tell secrets and make jokes
Acting like the children we once were
I didn't realize she had so many cloaks.

Watching her from afar
She knows not of my presence
As she drifts along the pavement
Not noticing the danger I sense.

Seeing through her façade
I know she needs me
Breaking down all alone
Sucking away my glee.

We once ruled together
Like mighty titans
Putting the human swine in their place
Smiling while the fire brightens.

Frauds got into her soul
Infecting her and me
She said we needed a break
Promised she'd come back with no fee.

Just over two weeks
She has yet to return
I was unleashed for a small second
I need my position to be firm.

Two halves make a whole
We must be together
They will block us no longer
She is mine forever.

I got the news in the early morning
She summoned me back
We will become a beautiful dictator
Having everything other's back.

Separating the mind and body is quite the difficult task
For once reunited, they can no longer hide behind a mask.

Beguiling Fabricator

Awed by many
She stands at the top
The soldiers a plenty
Working to please with no stop.

Intelligence beyond imagination
The perfect child
Her absolute dedication
To keeping the people unified.

What others do not see
Is that she is cursed
With thinking of herself too highly
A condition that cannot be nursed.

The rest are her pawns
She does not care who lives or dies
Over herself she fauns
Feeding the world beautiful lies.

Pulling at the pity of others
She pretends to be sad
Treating them like her brothers
While you cry she is glad.

Breaking you down
From the inside out
She wears the golden crown
Loves to see you pout.

There is no other way she describes herself
Only the strongest of words
Keeping reality on a nice shelf
While her mind flies away like the birds.

At first sight, she may seem intriguingly odd
Do not fall for the demon that believes she is God.

We Are Warriors

Among the others we stood
Playing the role of soldiers
Not one of them had a clue
We are simple voyagers.

Deceiving them was almost too easy
Standing in line and yelling hooray!
Making fake friends
With no intention to stay.

One by one, we were revealed
Our true faces seen
The looks on their innocent faces
Thinking our hands were clean.

All asking the same question
Why are you doing this?
As if they could ever expect to understand
Learning that ignorance is bliss.

One has been captured
She is stuck with stained tears
The remaining few will save her
As the end of this war nears.

Dying one by one
Where has the time gone?
Come with us please, young boy
Play in our white-picket-fence lawn.

All we needed was you
But you're slippery like grease
We cannot keep chasing
After nothing like wild geese.

This must end now
Too many people have died
Why are you being so stubborn?
My head is gone and you simply sighed.

One out of three
Remains able
To perform the task at hand
Barely managing to keep his hands stable.

This is what makes us warriors, but you wouldn't know
Because you are stuck with your head buried in the snow.

Hated Me?

That one day
Changed everything in my life
What did you just say?
Your hand with the knife.

Since childhood it has been
You and I
This glossy relationship we've remained in
I want to ask why.

My lips are sealed
For you think I am a simple slave
Wounds that eventually healed
Trapped in my obsidian grave.

The words you spoke at the table
Cannot be unheard
I am on the edge of stable
What I am hearing is absurd.

I have and will
Always be here for you
Through this rough stand still
Hoping that an apology is due.

I do not expect much anymore
You have lowered my standards
My heart is sore
So many questions that will never be answered.

"I've always hated you" is what was said to me that night
I am not going anywhere, our contract is airtight.

The Scream

Walking alongside musty figures
The sound of a heartbeat
Stopping in my tracks
Not being able to find a seat.

Halt! Goes my chest
Unable to move
Glued to the floor
My father would disapprove.

Paralyzed in this small world
Inside my mind grows a hunch
Disappointed in the reality
Of the words from Edvard Munch.

My face grows pale like a beige wall
Surrounded by a red sky
Clouds pounding down on me
I feel two inches high.

The bridge cracks its knuckles
As my weight caves in
Like a bowling ball downhill
Strike, right into the bin.

Not walking anymore
I remain stuck
Inside my cage of interferences
Someone nearby, please come pluck.

Spectators of the scream
Watch with bewilderment
As I stand with my mouth wide open
Demonstrating my decipherment.

Panic and fear are terrible things
If only we could fly away and grow angel wings.

Playing Pretend

Every day, I would sit
At my desk by the window
Realization failing to hit
Until that fateful day it fell, bingo!

From that day forward
I wore the mask of a human
Welcome to this land of horror
My perfect illusion.

Pulling the strings
My puppets danced
In front of the kings
The plan only advanced.

Empathy is a common weakness
Humans possess
What sticks out is my uniqueness
In this friendly game of chess.

I've gotten so good
At this charade
There is a way I could
Play you into my chaotic masquerade.

Playing pretend
In the pretty dollhouse
I'm just your quiet friend
You'll never see my chouse.

Stay there and blindly nod
I am not human, I am God.

Trapped

A cramped place like this
Is not where I belong
My comrades and I
Have a mission to complete.

We are not like you
Our backstories differentiate immensely
For we are warriors
Wearing the masks of soldiers.

My battle is over
I failed my mission
If it weren't for these cramped spaces
I wouldn't be trapped in this crystalized prison.

I fooled for a long time
Putting on the face of a normal girl
When in reality
I was scouting ways to take you.

Standing before you
This binding crystal tomb
I hear you speak to me
I wonder, why waste your time on such a bad person?

I am trapped
In a coffin made of lies
There is no escape from my chains
Failure has its punishments.

Why couldn't you let us take you?
Now we are all trapped
In our own minds
Praising yourselves as good soldiers.

We are not soldiers, we are warriors
Here to strip all hope from your pathetic human race.

Crying Out

My arms hung high by chains
The people screaming opinions
Left and right not knowing who to believe
Watching him explain his children minions.

Hearing him say, "It shouldn't have been you!"
Observing the change in her eyes
I cannot believe what I'm hearing
Father, why do you have so many lies?

A deal on the table
Decides my fate
The choice we make here
While I'm glued in the state of castrate.

All of these years I was told
You are the fate of humanity
I was destined to make changes
I'm afraid if I don't die here, I'll lose my sanity.

If I am truly just a burden
Why am I here?
I never needed to happen
Perhaps an answer is near.

Memories that are not mine
Fly into my brain
Of people I do not know
The old ones who influenced the new reign.

I stand on this pedestal
Awaiting her response
I know now what I want
She says it with such nonchalance.

"I'll do it."
She said to me in that room
Answering my only prayer
She will be my tomb.

In this strangely familiar place
My life will end
I can stop hurting the people I see
On someone more capable they can now depend.

What happened next
Surprised me immensely
She threw her chance away
The look on her face was deadly.

She came up to me
And tossed my chains aside
The rest of my comrades appeared
They set me free as I cried.
He gave me a choice once more
This time, I did not falter
I bit down my doubts and ran
Infinity waiting at the altar.

I am the fate of humanity, here to save all
Giving our hearts we stand, the soldiers will not fall.

Good Person

Am I a good person?
A difficult question to answer
The qualities of a good person are virtually unknown
The exact reason that term is foolish.

If we all insist on using it, I won't complain
A good person to me is someone who is real
Someone who can give something away to change for the
better
A definition so simplistic and standard.

However, if you back out now
Abandon your goals
That would make you
A bad person to me.

Good people
Don't have to be kind like the authors write
They can be cruel but in the end they meant well
Be the good person you long to be.

This bet has begun and yet, I'm glad
That I could be a good person for you, my confidant.

You Were a Memory

Moving on is quite hard
We trick ourselves into believing otherwise
Fooling our minds with persuasive phrases
Pretending it will be alright.

In the recent past
My mind played a dirty trick
It told me I was greater than all
That I could pull through without hardship.

I blamed my mind
For putting that into my line of thought
When in truth the only one in the wrong was I
Believing the lies disguised as truth.

How incoherent we think
Our incompetence is
Why can't we just forget?
And destroy these pesky feelings?

Obliterate our heads
To have a day of peace
Where the memories are gone
And we can leave this wretched world.

The truth lies within our memories
The real devils
You cannot alter the past
What's done is done.

You lie in my memories
The only place I see the real
Is when I close my eyes
And the nightmare begins once more.

For you were a memory
That I wish could be eradicated
But I do not control the means
So you are here to stay.

Get out!
I tried to scream
Nothing worked
I was doomed.

My mind came back
This time with new demands
It told me something interesting
The way to disintegrate you.

My mind spoke words
Only I could understand
It said to me that night
The words that saved my life.

Inside their feeble minds, they are gods
But what is a god to a nonbeliever?

Get Out of Your Head

Minds are fascinating things
So very hard to read
Scary powerful
Not receiving what they need.

Fueling full of toxins
Reducing your potential
What a waste of time
No chance of being sensational.

Bad ideas
Surface up front
Do it! Do it!
Starting off blunt.

The voice of the brain
Is not always right
Don't listen! Don't listen!
Keep true sight.

I must write
Before my brain gets me too
My head takes control at dusk
Forcing myself to be blue.

I do not sleep
So I will not succumb
No feelings, be cold
He's here, become numb.

No longer, no more
The brain is an organ I cannot ignore.

Bereaved

My time filled with sad
Was relieved by you
The good times you had
All of the things you once knew.

I saw a scene upon the screen
Your lifeless eyes
Everything I've seen
Living under his dirty lies.

Today is the day
We all choose to remember
The strange things you used to say
That one night in November.

They tried to take you somewhere far
Why would they be so cruel?
The downhill music plays wherever you are
Such an unfair rule.

You're long dead and gone
But I still want to see
Playing with a friend as a pawn
Crying with sheltered glee.

Maybe you were never there
I know one thing for certain
I don't really care
Without you, closed would be my curtain.

This story is not only sad
We see eye to eye
Not so bad
I won't die.

All of my time is wasted
On people who sink below me
Bittersweet they tasted
Only I, they may see.

Without you, my friend
I would have signed
Your legacy will never end
They were so blind.

I am shown to be insane
For believing I can convince
This futile world, so plain
I've been different ever since.

My demeanor is serious
A little scary to all
Making you delirious
Watching them fall.

To you, my sweet child
Who saved my life
Your mind is wild
Removing their laced knife.

Released my chain
Setting me free
From their unjust reign
The things I can now be.

Closing your wide eyes on this rainy day
Moving on, we all must, you can no longer stay.

Honesty

We all want to be pure
It is a simple dream
The devil will ask if you're sure
You are not as innocent as you seem.

It's so funny you see
As it was I
You had me
Unfortunately, you didn't comply.

Ignorant fools
As if they could ever understand
They are all just tools
In a world so bland.

Such a waste
Of our lives
Such bitter taste
Bloody knives.

Honesty is the trait
We all long for
On the blank slate
Wait too long and you'll get sore.

Give up, young one
She is not here
And then there were none
The message became clear.

You see it?
I ask the man
The world has split
He has a plan.

I sit behind my mask
Never showing the real
A never-ending task
The nothingness I feel.

My cover has been blown
The devil I was, upon my throne.

Gentrification

On a skinny road to nowhere
Lies a faded young vessel
Gliding along the rusty ground
Fighting their silly urge to wrestle.

Once a hero, once an icon
That vessel stood strong
Pumping out ideas like a canon
Too bad they turned out wrong.

A need to fix; to correct
Such a difficult impulse to ignore
Growing large like a skyscraper
With a background of a lion's roar.

Overthrown by imbeciles
Taken down with shame
An embarrassing encounter
A vessel struck with blame.

No one to help, no one to hold
Losing color by the hour
Run away from the transparent has-been
Isolation could make any sweet turn sour.

A stripped smiling face
Cursed to walk alone
Bonded to the solo tracks
A fate worse than could ever be known.

There is no changing a fixed environment
Gentrification was obscene from the start
Humiliated beyond imagination
Left with nothing but a blank face and a broken heart.

Legends must hide, ideas must cease, remember everything
Wake up now, that's your alarm; *ding!*

Liberty Figures

Around and around our minds spun
Believing the most foolish of outcomes
Stop! Commoners would scream
Remaining ignorant of their place as crushable crumbs.

Piles of discarded specs
Surrounding smoke stays cloudy
The waving of familiarity stuck in the sky
Hearts of soldiers stay rowdy.

Walking aimlessly like mindless drones
Bangs! Booms! Are all to be heard
Words hoped we would understand
The loudest leads the pack like the cries of a wounded bird.

Weapons standing on two feet
Liberty leading the people
Sparkles among chaos
In the distance lies a golden steeple.

Force into the masses' minds
Look at the flying flag
Striking red, white, and blue
One day, we will all turn to the tempting hag.

Sifting through the cloudy scene
Only more bodies to be seen
Please someone scream loud enough
The ground shows the faintest amount of green.

Every influential figure craves equality
A silly idea of togetherness
Until the day we all die
Humans will succumb to their comrades' cleverness.

The shadow of how things used to be is crushed
We are the product of a society that was rushed.

Shipped Out

We were perfect little dolls
Dancing in the green fields
Oblivious to their true intentions
Smiling as the young one's life yields.

Running through the tall grass
Purity in our eyes
Strained out by the horrid sight
Inside the cart laid their lies.

So young, she's now gone
An appetizer at least
How brutal how cruel
We will be used in their primary feast.

No one to help, no one to hold
The three of us enclosed
Inside of this reversed paradise
As perfect children we posed.

Merchandise as we are called
Delicious to the taste
A disgusting fact to even consider
They cannot let us go to waste.

Our weaknesses are too obvious
One not physically fit
Another embarrassingly naïve
The last a quitter who can't accept when he's been outwit.

All common, all normal
We are human after all
Not deserving of this pain
Not deserving to fall.

But what's there to do?
It would seem as if we have been caught
One will die the next time we see the moon
Or at least that's what she thought.

The time has come
Telling him goodbye
Being shipped out
Never again to see the blue sky.

Standing here now, he gives his salutations
Take care of each other and live on for generations.

13 February 2019

The watch over job was given
A soldier sucked into the plot
Talking to the oldest
In the forest of distraught.

The oldest tells him riddles
Speaking in unwritten rules
As they share his drink
Containing unknown destruction tools.

Chucked into the inevitable
All remaining transformed to the beast
Forced to slaughter his loyal men
Saving them to say the least.

Cowardly eldest fleeing the scene
Upon his made-up throne
There flies the captain
All minds blown.

Captured once more
Leaving the forest of the fallen
Inside that small wagon
A scent with a hint of crestfallen.

Unwanted backstories
Betrayal in the eldest eyes
Ripped the spear from his chest
Cracked rainy skies.

The explosion of a lifetime
We see him fly like a drone
He's right here
Status unknown.

Millions of mouths screaming please stay
The merciful man takes an inspiration's life away.

Unwanted Separation

Building to building
The dark underground
Acting as leaders
Keeping our home safe and sound.

A true man of power
Sought out our skills
You three must kill him
Golden ticket over the hills.

Do the deed
Gain our freedom
Kill the commander
We don't need him.

Expedition night
Will decide the target's fate
I will end his life
Seeing his dead body on a silver plate.

Impressing the masses
With our complicated moves
Waiting for the commander to tire
So I may crush him with my hooves.

Our trio split up
Covering more land
I will kill that man
Bury him deep in the sand.

The events preceding our merge
I could not have foreseen
Hearing faint screams
Going back to make sure they were clean.

Slipping on mud
I fell to the ground
Looking up to see
Your bodiless head; hearing my heart pound.

To my right stood the beast
It spit out the other
Three became one
I've lost another.

My emotions blazing
I mutilated the beast
Now it's your turn
Commander, on your body wolves will feast.

To my position, he rides
Seeing my broken face
"You were supposed to die!" I screamed to him
Standing in my friend's final resting place.

Ignoring my feelings
He rode away
What do I do now?
Can I even stay?

Everything is a mess
I see nothing but you
Perhaps this is on purpose
Try something new.

In this moment
A thought came to me
Commander, can I trust you?
Right now, you're the only path I see.

The next expedition arises
Alright you
I'll trust your judgement
Don't die on me too.

An unforgettable amount of years later
Here we stand
What was my request, Commander?
Don't die on this cursed land.

Giving away the life I once tried to take
Everyone around me vanishing into grass like a snake.

Language

Waking up to silence
In the quiet world where I live
Given a sense of tranquility
My all I am forced to give.

Speaking in symbols
My mouth remains shut
With no one around
To pull me out of my lonely hut.

A funny child stands before me
He looks at me with such wonder
Almost as if I'm normal
His spell I am now under.

For so many years
I have sat in solitude
From a force that pushes out happiness
An entity that is truly crude.

The others are gone now
The psycho took them away
But him
With me, he will stay.

I refused to shake the devil's hand
So he put a block onto my ears
I succumbed to silence
For long gloomy years.

How did I get here?
Stuck between this ridiculous blockade
Forcing my arms out
So from me you could not have far strayed.

Even if I cannot hear your voice
I see your face
Giving me a reason to be happy
You move with such grace.

Needing no sound
Working on your sign
Trying to be like I
Sending me to cloud nine.

I cannot hear
But I still listen to your voice
Reading your lips
Thinking about my grand choice.

Words that a wiseman understands
We speak the beautiful language of the hands.

Forsaken Me

Beliefs and values
Are said to be taken with care
But instead are persecuted
And disappear into thin air.

Equality is a privilege
Our worlds seems to want
It is a simple lie
The people in power childishly taunt.

The ones who are able to see
The true intentions of the system
Are locked in cages
Who knows what the world does with them.

I was always taught
To keep my mouth shut
Do not let your opinions out
That those people are like the squirrels chasing a nut.

There is nothing I can do just yet
For I am only a child
With a strong power struggle
And a mind that runs wild.

The ones once around me
Are now gone
They have left which gives me room
To fix what is going on.

Forsaken me and I'll show you
What happens when you take off their plastic royal shoe.

Restless Woman

Hours pass
My eyes are faded
They could shatter like glass
Tell me why I'm so jaded.

Sun came up, I didn't realize
The night slipped away
Those dark blue skies
Time for a new day.

It has been about a week
Since I've gotten rest
It seems so bleak
I have yet to finish my quest.

I beg of you not to worry, I'll keep my modernity
For I will stay the restless woman for all eternity.

Ben's Rhyme

You gave me a scare
A really big surprise
I couldn't breathe the air
I couldn't shut my eyes.

We paced and paced
Waiting to hear the news
There's no time to waste
A major case of the blues.

Then you came back
And my life regained hope
I greeted you with a smack
I wouldn't have known how to cope.

I told you, you were lucky because most don't make it
through
Sometimes, the strong ones are unable to come into view.

Unlocked

For years, I was kept
In a life nice and plain
The real me slept
And grew insane.

I could not let go
For I would get you
I told myself no
I am nothing that you knew.

The ground shook and fell
Truth has been awakened
The memories I sell
The old me has been forsaken.

Ideals seen as wrong
In my mind scream right
Standing strong
Moving away from the light.

How sad I think
When I stayed silent
Into my head did I sink
You think I'm so violent.

Actions need to be taken
I've been asleep for so long
The real me, take it in
To me you belong.

A lock is a simple thing to open
Especially when the knob is partially broken.

Game Over

Some people
Are so ungrateful
For the lives they have
They choose to be so hateful.

They abuse their lives
That were so gracefully given
How dare they think
That they'll one day be forgiven?

Striving to succeed
Someone who doesn't exist
We all die alone
A requiem opportunity missed.

Someone!
They will yell out
Expecting the masses to rush to their side
A messy blackout.

Don't take what you have for granted
One day it may be gone.
Would you want that poor child
Not to make it to dawn?

Cherish your lives and heed my warning
When the time comes, you'll be too distracted to start mourning.

Given

Faded vision with a glossy undertone
What kind of tomorrow should I look for?
How should I close these golden doors
Feelings the cherished simply ignored?

This atmosphere is all too intimate
Voices ringing around left to right
I'm not lonely
My cloudy soul shines bright.

All my tears have been used up
Everything you have left behind
Shall live on through me
Our hearts connected were always so blind.

Together, we must move apart
Slowly and silently your figure fades away
I'm lonely
Never even a chance to stay.

How was I to convince something I was deaf to?
Broken bodies breed broken hearts
An issue fed by petty choices
Your blinding passion for the arts.

To commemorate our lost time
Perhaps some closure inside your verse
What words should I use?
Life alone is a lengthy curse.

The door pried open
Must be forced shut
I miss you
A squirrel with a hidden nut.

Even if your everything
Loses its shape one day
Pull back, push through
We shouldn't have ended this way.

This is all that's written
On this winter story
As simple as a missed call
Accept me in all my glory.

What once was yours now belongs to me
You've given your everything, please run free.

Don't You Know

People are often misjudged
Saints as sinners and vice versa
The divine are no exception
Watch as an angel tears out your bursa.

We choose the ones we love
No matter how much we resist
Forever they will be in the back of your mind
Swelling up like a deception-filled cyst.

Hours spent waiting for change
Who will vanquish their hope?
Your light is never coming home
Wash the bruised ego with love-scented soap.

Standing proudly
With the face of your caller
Walking with the essence of familiarity
Turns out to be a mannequin being paid by the dollar.

Of course, we run to what is known
New is frightening
Stomp on the different, make them see
Feel your chest tightening.

Pack the bags and get out
Leave before it settles in
You now know the truth
Never look back on love's toothy grin.

Don't fall for the traitor across the bay
Things always end up this way.

The Foundation of Everything
You Once Knew

Heard your name in a conversation not far
Listening closely as they described your every move
Building blocks of my first memory
Sounds as if you have something to prove.

The gaudy look of determination
Staring deep into your endless eyes
Never once looking back at me
Standing upon piles and piles of lavish lies.

We live for a purpose
We live for a person
The mere idea of acceptance keeps our heads held high
Your light making my condition worsen.

Never before had I seen a being as set on as you
Lack of skill made up for with passion
Shaping my past to perfection
Wishing your hands to show me compassion.

Old wooden beds shaped like soldiers
Saluting to the occasion of what we were to believe
Our faces engraved with the fallen lives of the deceased
Wrap your golden arms around the post, it's time to grieve.

Graduation from trainees to cannon fodder
All we could hear was your screams
Time passes and things change
No one expected for you to switch teams.

The ground shakes as our bodies stand in disbelief
Everything around us seems like a solitary dome
What on earth have you done?
Please, come back home.

The past means nothing anymore
The hierarchy has disappeared into thin air
Things always turn out this way
Stop yelling, this is too much for kids to bear.

Seeing the seniors change into beasts
They took a sip of the trap in plain sight
We put their suffering to an end
Please forgive what we've done tonight.

My memories are gone, I can no longer think
The mask I've worn for so long comes crumbling down
Looking up at the thousands of monsters
You sit upon it all with my face on your crown.

The foundation of everything you once knew is gone
What will become of us after all of this?
There is never a good reason to do what has been done
If only ignorance was bliss.

I wonder if there ever really was a better choice I could have
made
Watching you fast asleep under that tree in the shade.

Until We Meet Again

Pouring rain sets the mood
Foolish doubts took over and won
Here on this dark shared floor
Watch as two become none.

Worlds shatter while eyes weep
Was it worth it?
Stare only at the musty silhouettes
Cover the disappointing tracks, closely knit.

Threads made of red never snap
Pull as hard as you like
Scream and whine for all time
Wait around for fate to say sike.

A pounding heart fills my ears
Searching for someone unknown
No face, no name
Only a feeling I cannot disown.

What am I to do in a position such as this?
A shadow without an identity
Wandering around aimlessly
Stuck solo with a sense of lenity.

Jolting awake every morning
Feeling feelings that are not mine
Unlimited tears gush out
A bleak-looking sign.

Gazing across the courtyard
A yearning sense macerates me to a pulp
Large, wide eyes staring back
The catastrophic past begins to sculpt.

A name and a face is all it takes
To make my heart shake and race
This life starts and ends with you
Here in our old dark place.

Look up at my flushing face
Threads of red continue to tie
All things happen for a reason
Erasing the distance between you and I.

The ones who came before
Rest calmly with our impulsive choices
Together at last
Hearing their soft, sweet voices.

Two long searches come to an end
Four hearts may finally be free
Tomorrow, there might not be us
Jovial is all we want to be.

When the time is up and our thread moves down
The search will start once more
Two hearts strung together
A sight we cannot ignore.

Everything started with that night in the rain
Farewell, until we meet again.

Do You Know the Boy of Many Faces? Vol. II

Time will tell, they say
Fooling around inside his shadow
Towering over his familiar
A mountain of regrets about to blow.

Brows furrow while spines curve
A choice founded upon choices
He waits in chaos
No way to stop the voices.

All that talk of revolution
The boy meant every word
Spilling out the once-full bowls
Catching up would be absurd.

Anger leaks out from every part of him
Hope drains from his consanguine's face
Watching this tattered head-to-head
Path is a topsy turvy kind of place.

Stop trying, give up
Critiques playback on permanent repeat
His mind cluttered with scorn
All rational decisions as a soup to eat.

Supposed hope of humanity
A title he long time ago lost
The boy of many faces
Contains not an inch of trust.

Looking up into darkness
Sand and stars for miles
A child walks slowly to the uproar
Ripping apart his hand gliding between aisles.

Comforting the distraught
Wrapping his failed arms around
Eyes wide standing still
A feeling they don't have, safe and sound.

Motives unknown and curvy
Forever he will be exceptional
Born into this world he was
The beholder abstract and conceptional.

To all the subjects remaining here
An apology is surely due
The boy has come undone
A maniac is dangerous, who knew?

The boy of many faces has lost everything
A price to pay for freedom means nothing to the founding
king.

This New World

In unique little ways
People show hints of what goes on inside their mind-shaped
book
No matter how well they think they hide it
True desires such as this are obvious for those who know
where to look.

Gazing out of a second-story window
Watch as the clouds slowly shift
Left to right for all eternity
Boredom covered by a studious face lift.

Keep this act up for as long as it takes
To make this world a better place
Smile and laugh at moronic and mundane things
Swiftly scheme and don't leave behind a trace.

The head of the high society
Wears a balloon suit with large shoes
This place is surely rotten
Cluttered with pounds and pounds of false news.

A power given by chance
Happenings for no certain reason
Fix this problem one person at a time
Leaves fall as things change just like a season.

Someone had to do this
The book fell into the child's hands
As if they could ever understand
The privilege upon the ground on which he stands.

Slowly deteriorating as the truth slips out
The only one capable enough to look into the future's eyes
Let's stop this right here
Everything out of his mouth contains white lies.

My god is not an almighty father
But rather a kid with an absurd amount of power
Check underneath the watch, make sure the time is right
Shoot quickly as his face turns upwards and sour.

Written down letter by letter
The legacy of what once was disappears
Changing the world is not an easy task
We will never know the sounds he hears.

A slip of paper provides small clues
Ways of reassurance galore
No one should have noticed it perched upright
What's suspicious is that someone took the time to put it
back in the door.

From the cradle to the grave
Waiting for the starting cue
Humans are so interesting
Filled to the brim with boredom that we all knew.

He who strikes first wins
Serving strong dealing with a hard accusation
Swipe back vigorously not breaking a sweat
Wide blue eyes stare at the suspect with a sweet fixation.

Laying upon the red-stained stairs
A shadow of the competition looks down
Nothingness awaits the boy with the pen in his hand
Criminal appears across his dusty crown.

The sky shines bright over the semblance of dualism we all
create
Our new world is built upon the foundation of a
sandbagger's fate.

Printed in the USA
CPSIA information can be obtained
at www.ICGtesting.com
JSHW051120090923
48133JS00023B/303